CALICO and BEYOND:
The Use of Patterned Fabric in Quilts

CALICO and BEYOND:

The Use of Patterned Fabric in Quilts

Roberta Horton

C&T Publishing
Lafayette, California

Copyright © 1986 by Roberta Horton.

Cover: Pieced and Patched Stars
49″ × 58″
Roberta Horton

Photography by Lynn Kellner and Sharon Risedorph.
Kellner/Risedorph Photography
761 Clementina
San Francisco, CA 94103
415/431-5851

Design by Bobbi Sloan

Published by
C&T Publishing
P.O. Box 1456
Lafayette, CA 94549

ISBN: 0-914881-03-5

Library of Congress Catalog Card No.: 85-72039

Printed in the United States of America

✳

*To George McLeod Peterson, Adelaide Peterson Mashuta,
and Cynthia Michael Horton — my grandmother, mother, and daughter.
May the quilting thread remain unbroken between the generations.*

CONTENTS

FOREWORD

The purpose of this book is to help quiltmakers understand patterned fabric, that is, fabric with a printed or woven design on it. Once you understand what you're looking at, you can begin to gain the knowledge of how best to use it. Then you no longer have to take the safe approach when selecting fabric for your quilts.

I began teaching quiltmaking in 1972. The exercises in this book are based on various classes and workshops I have developed since then. Each class contributed a piece to the giant puzzle of my understanding of patterned fabric.

My class on the selection and use of prints (see Lesson 1) came first. It was developed to provide a general understanding of printed fabric to quiltmakers, whether at a beginning or advanced level.

I became interested in Japanese fabric when one of my adult education classes made a Japanese family crest quilt in 1976. I investigated a local store that specialized in Japanese fabric and was immediately intrigued with the fabric and how I might use it in my own work. The section of Japanese patchwork (see Lesson 4) represents the culmination of my personal struggle to work with this alien fabric. It wasn't until 1982 that I developed a class focusing on Japanese patchwork. Then I really began to learn!

My interest in Afro-American quilts (see Lesson 5) stems from a magazine notice of a 1981 quilt show. Up until that time, I hadn't been aware of this type of quilt. Tracking down information on these unusual quilts has been a real challenge; ultimately, teaching about Afro-American quilts became part of my "Great American Scrap Quilt" class.

The development and teaching of the Japanese patchwork class triggered my renewal of interest in traditional scrap quilts. While doing a workshop on this subject in Reno, Nevada, I watched the students working with the problems of using nontraditional fabric to execute a traditional quilt pattern. As I gave them suggestions, I suddenly felt I had found the key to understanding scrap quilts. I knew then I would develop a class on this subject (see Lessons 2 and 3). I also felt I had come full circle in my interests because antique scrap quilts had long held my attention but I had never felt I fully understood them.

You may have noticed in the above discussion that the lessons are not listed in the order of their appearance in this book. Their order here represents the time sequence of my interest, proving that we often don't work in a straight line when exploring a subject. I tend to work on several thoughts at once, rather than focusing on only one thing at a time. (During this same period I was also very involved with Amish quilts, and the use of solid colors in quilts. My book, *An Amish Adventure: A Workbook for Color in Quilts,* grew out of this interest.)

The sequence I have chosen for this book represents a more logical order, going from simple to complex. I suggest that you move through this book from beginning to end, doing all the exercises. You'll be amazed at the increased understanding of patterned fabric you will gain from the experience.

Acknowledgments

Again, a thank you to all those who had to quilt like crazy to meet the deadline. And thanks to those who had the foresight to take the classes early on and whose work then served as an inspiration for those who followed. A special note of gratitude to Scott Robson and Dr. Maude Wahlman for their photographs and help.

INTRODUCTION

When I was in the fifth grade, I was told I shouldn't wear small prints because I was tall but instead should restrict myself to large-scale prints. How I hungered for small prints. And I felt guilty every time I wore a forbidden tiny print. Probably one of the reasons I became a quiltmaker was to give me an excuse to buy those small prints I had been prohibited from using.

For the first five years or so of my quilting career I limited myself to small calico prints. Initially they were hard to find because quilt stores hadn't yet come into existence and manufacturers hadn't begun to cater to the world of quiltmakers. As the desired fabric became more plentiful, I found myself becoming sated on a steady diet of little prints. I began to experiment with other types of patterned fabric.

I have always loved fabric and I find that looking at it and purchasing it starts my creative juices flowing. Sometimes I have a specific project in mind. Other times, I'm just adding to my collection. In fact, I have finally come to realize it's an unrealistic goal to use up all the fabric I own. It's enough that a fabric sparks my creativity, whether or not I actually use it in a project.

As a quiltmaker, I generally buy small amounts of fabric (½ yard) because I grow tired of a fabric when I see too much of it. Once I use a fabric, I may never include it in another project, even though some is left over. Some small gift fragments are saved and it always gives me great pleasure when I finally use them. I savor them all the more for the small amount that appears in the project.

Buying only a little bit of fabric also means the excitement of running out. Over the years, I have discovered that projects in which I have used up a particular fabric and been forced to substitute prove to be far more interesting when they are completed. These are the quilts that seem to hold my interest, or, to borrow a marketing term, to have a long shelf life.

Why do some quiltmakers insist on attempting to match a fabric if they run out? Many times I have seen a small fragment tacked up at a quilt store along with a plea for matching fabric from someone else's collection. I finally realized the answer is because it's safe. That quiltmaker doesn't have the nerve to make a substitution because she fears it might ruin the appearance of the entire quilt.

Just the opposite is true. Too many of us are overworking our quilts. In our quest for the perfect quilt, we think we must plan and control every aspect of the quilt. Perhaps the truth is we don't really understand how to use patterned fabric. An exciting use of fabric has the potential to make our quilts more interesting to the viewer. That is the goal of this book.

I have purposely not included a historical treatment of textile design and technology here because the subject is very complex and not really necessary for understanding the use of fabric. Likewise, I haven't included patterns or sewing techniques since many good books are available specifically on these subjects. What I feel I can contribute here is a better understanding of patterned fabric and its use in our quilts.

1

Defining Categories

Quiltmakers need to think of their fabric as a collection. Giving your accumulated fabrics an official title changes how you think about them and how others perceive them. Remember, for a quiltmaker, fabric represents a creative medium. A painter has tubes of paint, a potter bags of clay. A quiltmaker must have a varied collection of fabric in order to create quilts.

It's important to divide your fabric collection into categories, and to inventory the individual categories. Some will be complete; you have adequate examples. Other categories may be seriously lacking; you need to be on the lookout for examples to fill in the void. A fabric collection cannot be a static accumulation.

When a designer creates a new piece of fabric, numerous decisions about the design elements are made. These decisions are the recipe for printing that fabric. As cooks, we sometimes discover a new spice we haven't worked with before. Enthralled with the taste, we add it to everything. Eventually everything tastes alike and we grow tired of that spice. We have made its use so ubiquitous that we have lost our fascination with it. Similarly, the average quiltmaker keeps buying the same fabric over and over again. The overused fabric acts much the same as the overused spice in our recipes. Then we wonder why our quilts are boring. They don't seem to have any zest.

A quiltmaker with a good collection of fabric—one with many categories—can create quilts that will sustain the viewer's interest. Quiltmakers should therefore take fabric collecting seriously. The purpose of this section is to show you different ways to look at your fabric—to divide it into categories. (Throughout this lesson, I will be dealing only with patterned fabric.)

Hue

Hue means color. The easiest way to store fabric is by color: all the fabrics of one hue can be stacked or placed together, with solids separated from prints. I establish categories based on the primary colors of red, yellow, and blue and the secondary colors of orange, green, and purple. Refer to the color wheel in Figure 1.1.

The tertiary colors fall between the primary and secondary colors; their names are composed of both terms, such as blue-green or yellow-green. (A blue-green might be called aqua or turquoise, but it's easier to just call it blue-green.) I mainly stack according to the primary and secondary colors. When I go to choose a particular piece of fabric, I make the decision as to whether I want a blue-green or a yellow-green from within my green pile. If I have a large assortment of a particular tertiary color, I keep those fabrics together and insert them into the correct color order.

There are also the neutral colors—black, white, grey, and brown, which includes tans and beiges. These have their own separate piles. If a white patterned fabric is a print featuring a color, then it is placed into the appropriate color pile. If it's a white-on-white print or pattern (like a damask weave) that gives the design feeling, then I make a separate pile within my neutrals for it. Neutrals can be added to any color scheme without changing it. They are a way of stretching out that color.

Some printed fabrics contain several colors. View the overall effect when seen at a distance to determine the correct color pile for storage.

There are many ways to tackle color within a

quilt. I find it helpful to understand three of the color schemes:

Monochromatic: One hue is used. Different values can be included of that one hue. White added to a hue lightens it and black darkens it. A monochromatic scheme for red could therefore include pink, red, and maroon. The neutrals may be added without altering the fact that the scheme is monochromatic.

Analogous: Hues close together on the color wheel are combined. When selecting the related colors, go less than halfway around the color wheel. Red could therefore be combined with purple and blue, or blue could be combined with blue-green, green, and purple. The values may vary and the neutrals can also be added. I find this color scheme richer than monochromatic.

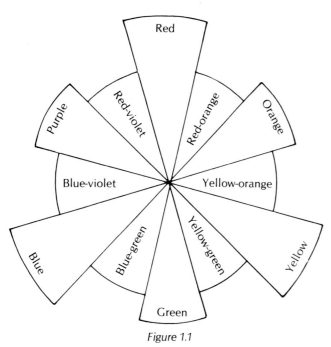

Figure 1.1

Contrasting: Hues opposite each other on the color wheel are combined. Accenting a hue with its contrast makes the hue richer, a more intense version of itself. A little rust (orange) thrown into a previously all blue quilt can rescue it from being boring. Constrasts used in equal amounts can be very dramatic, even loud. Picture the red and green of Christmas.

More color schemes are possible, but I find understanding these three gives a quiltmaker sufficient information to make a pleasing quilt. Once you select one patterned fabric, you have three ways to proceed: add more of that hue, add hues close by, or add the opposite hue. Different values can be used for depth and the neutrals can be added to stretch out the color.

There's one last important concept to consider about color. *Quilters tend to overmatch.* When purchasing fabric for a specific project, we often think that each individual piece of yardage should carefully match the others of that hue. Quiltmakers have been known to scold the shopowner if she doesn't carry all the variations of one line made by a specific manufacturer so that the colors and even the dye lots can be identical. When lining up the bolts of fabric, we want them to be "pretty" together. In our minds, one of the requirements for pretty is matching.

Actually, the opposite is true. When fabrics are carefully matched as to hue, they blend together too much when combined. They appear as one piece of yardage rather than individual pieces and the composition looks flat. Take, for example, a log cabin quilt block. When you stitch the strips together for the dark side of the block, if too carefully matched, the finished result will read as one piece of fabric rather than joined strips. Why bother to do all the individual cutting and sewing if the finished result doesn't show it? See Figure 1.2 for an example of too careful matching.

Value

Value means the degree of lightness or darkness of a color. Basically fabrics have light, medium, or dark value. To determine the general value of a patterned fabric, look at the background color. In most cases, this will control the value of the piece. If the printed design area occupies the major portion of the available space, however, it may suggest the value for the fabric. Remember that prints with little value difference between the foreground and background will read as a solid from afar (Figure 1.3).

Two approaches can help you to determine value: you can try squinting your eyes, or you can use a reducing glass. This tool looks like a magnifying glass but reduces rather than enlarges. Reduction concentrates or exaggerates what is seen so the value will be more obvious. It's particularly helpful when you have several fabrics of very similar value and you want to determine which will read as the lightest or darkest.

The value of a fabric can be altered by over-dyeing it. Tea makes a subtle change, sometimes giving the fabric an antique appearance. It also helps to reduce the difference between the lightest and darkest elements. For example, white appears larger to our eyes than it actually is. When small areas of white are used in a design, sometimes a spotty, distracting appearance is the result. A reducing glass will alert you to this possibility, and tea dyeing can be the solution to the problem. (See the Appendix for a tea dyeing formula.)

High contrast fabrics can also be over-dyed with commercial dyes for a more dramatic change. Reserve

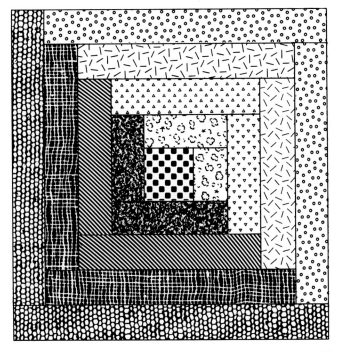

Poor Contrast

Figure 1.2

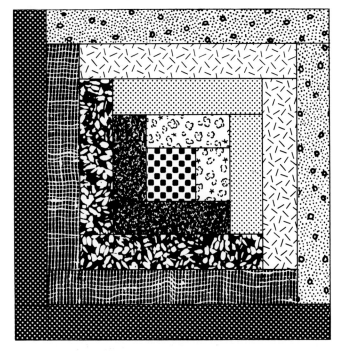

Good Contrast

Reads Light

Reads Medium

Reads Solid

Figure 1.3

this procedure for fabrics you really don't like and are considering giving away. You may be pleasantly surprised at the results. If you weren't going to use the fabric anyway, you haven't lost anything; if it works, consider it a positive recycling experience.

Value establishes pattern. Most quiltmakers think that color is what establishes the pattern in a block or a whole quilt. Actually, the value contrast between the colors provides the pattern. We only see the barn raising arrrangement of a log cabin quilt because there's a dark and light diagonal division of the individual blocks. These blocks placed together in a certain arrangement give us the pattern we recognize as barn raising.

Value differences suggest depth. Generally, light comes toward the viewer and dark recedes. Or you can make the opposite happen. The important thing to remember is that light and dark values aren't perceived on the same visual plane. Therefore, we can work with differing values within a quilt to enhance the depth of field. The special visual effects present in many contemporary quilts are achieved through a creative use of value.

Value is relative. Not until a fabric is inserted into its proper position in a project can we be sure of its value. For example, a fabric can be the light in one block and the medium in another. The value of a particular piece of fabric is dependent on the lightness and darkness of the other fabrics used with it. (See Figure 1.4.)

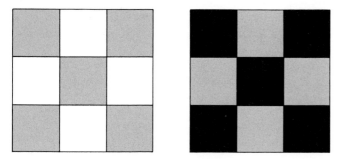

Figure 1.4

The value of our original fabric can also be altered within the project by changing the value of the surrounding fabric. If you darken the surrounding fabric, your fabric appears lighter. If the surrounding fabric is lightened, your fabric becomes darker (Figure 1.5).

 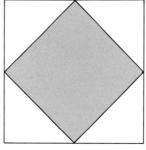

Lightens   *Figure 1.5*   Darkens

This is a good reason for doing some experimenting before your final decisions are made. When you've cut out the pieces for a block, lay them out as they will look when sewn and see what effect you're getting. This is best done if the pieces can be placed on a

pinup board. Stand back, or use the reducing glass, and study the result. Looking at bolts of fabric at the store or pieces of yardage in your studio won't tell you what the fabrics will do when they are actually combined.

One last word about value: *quiltmakers tend to buy one value.* In order for a quilt pattern to read successfully, you should combine different values within the project. If all your fabric were divided into piles of light, medium, and dark values, you would probably find a preponderance of one value. Recognize your buying bias, and make a conscious effort to purchase the lacking value or values. Dark background prints are produced in five times the quantity of light background prints. If you find it difficult to obtain light value prints, inspect the backs of the darks. Often they are usable as lights and can give a soft, muted look to the quilt. (See Photo 4A.)

Scale

Scale refers to the size of the patterned design on the fabric. There's an "average" calico print size. When I first became a quiltmaker, these were hard to find, but they're now made in abundance. They're easy to work with because the designs fit within the individual pattern shapes of our quilts. If you work with only one size print, however, you may find that your quilts develop a feeling of sameness and you'll quickly become bored with them (Figure 1.6).

When you study old quilts, you'll discover their makers often didn't limit their fabric choices to just one size print. This is particularly true of quilts made before 1840. Once the roller printing method became widespread, there was more of a sameness to the size of the prints.

Prints that are smaller than average read as a solid from afar, even if there's a high contrast between

Figure 1.6

the print and the background. Because they're viewed as a solid, their presence is a pleasant surprise when the quilt is inspected at close range. Very small-scale prints provide a pleasing contrast when paired with the average size calico.

Large-scale prints can also add excitement to your quilts, providing a welcome contrast when combined with the average calico or print size. However, few quilters consider using very large-scale prints, that is, prints in which the design can't be contained, or seen in its entirety, within an individual pattern shape. Rather than this being a disadvantage, it can work in your favor. Because of the large scale, you can't anticipate exactly what will appear within the shape or what it will include as to color and value. This opens up the possibility of some very pleasant surprises. Lesson 4 deals with working with nontraditional prints, and will explore this possibility further.

In summary, let's look at one type of print—dotted fabric—and see how scale affects its use. Fabric featuring dots requires careful thought before its use in quiltmaking. The dots will appear spotty if there's a great deal of contrast between the dots and the background value. This can make them harder to work with. Over-dyeing might be a solution if the spotting is a nuisance. Sometimes the spotty effect can work to your advantage by adding a sparkling affect, like twinkling stars. Dotted fabric comes with various sized dots; micro dots are the smallest. (See Figure 1.7.) Because the dot is so small, the fabric almost reads as a solid which makes it very easy to use. In fact, some quilters tend to overuse it. Beware of micro dot over-kill! Too much of anything is boring. Consider also using very large polka dots, where you capture only part of the design. This can be quite exciting. Remember that the smooth, round shape of dots can present a pleasing contrast to the details of tiny flowers and the straight lines of stripes and plaids. Study Photo 14B.

Density

Density refers to the proximity of the design elements to each other. Some fabrics are very tightly packed and others have a very spacious, airy appearance. Quiltmakers tend to buy one or the other. Here again, contrast is what adds interest. Our eyes flow smoothly over things that we perceive as similar. When there is something different to see, our eyes slow down and study the difference. Remember, one of the goals is to get the viewers caught up in the quilt. Their eyes have to be forced to slow down and view the individual parts (Figure 1.8).

Same Density

Same Density

Contrasting Density

Figure 1.8

Figure 1.7

Number of Colors Used in a Print

In order for a fabric to show a pattern, there has to be at least a light and dark of one hue or two different hues used. In general, the fewer the number of hues, the easier the fabric is to work with. This is because of fusion. At close range, our eyes can perceive the individual colors. The further away we move, the more we lose this ability and at some point, all the colors blend to give an all-over color. If many colors are present in the print, this new color may not even physically be present in the fabric. Quiltmakers sometimes get into trouble because of this fusion, since we don't consider what the fabric will look like in the finished project when viewed from afar. Again, a reducing glass will indicate this in advance. Another method is to back away from your fabric and view it from a distance when you're selecting it.

Multicolor prints tend to give a busy feeling because all the colors vie for attention. In fact, beginning quiltmakers tend to buy multicolor prints because they attract their attention on a shelf of fabric bolts. When actually combining prints, however, all this activity can be a disadvantage, particularly if most of the prints fall within this category. The more simple one- or two-color prints are much more subtle. They may not be as eye-catching, but they combine more effortlessly. Just remember to use multicolor prints sparingly. When included, they can suggest other colors to be added. They can also be added when a project is appearing too boring or lifeless.

One last thought on the colors used within a print. Most of us are too caught up in matching, as I mentioned earlier. Don't be concerned if, for example, the leaves in all your prints aren't exactly the same green. Remember that different greens, such as blue-greens and yellow-greens, represent colors that are close together on the color wheel, and are therefore an analogous color scheme. This difference in color will actually add some excitement to the project.

Design Layout

Design layout refers to the type of formula the artist uses to create the shapes on the fabric. The most common designs used for calicoes are the all-over and the repeat. An all-over design meanders over the fabric, with its elements often flowing together. There's usually a close density. A repeat design features a single shape which is rhythmically printed to form rows which can be parallel, offset, or diagonal. Be aware of these rows because their presence can be a shock in the completed project. There is space between the elements, giving the feeling of a low density. (See Figure 1.9.)

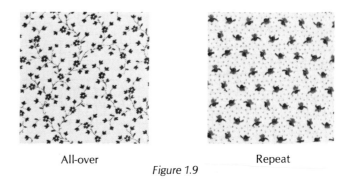

All-over   *Figure 1.9*   Repeat

Quilters usually show a preference for repeats or all-overs in their collection. When combining prints, here again contrast proves the most interesting (Figure 1.10).

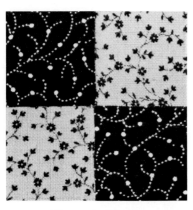  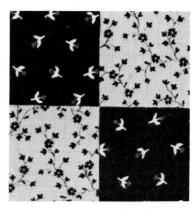

All-over + All-over   Repeat + Repeat   All-over + Repeat

Figure 1.10

Figure 1.11

Since most calico prints are floral, with curved, wavy-lined elements, I'd like to suggest geometrics as a separate design layout category. The bolder, straight-lined geometrics are generally thought of as more masculine and the florals as feminine. In fact, some of us only think of including geometrics when making a quilt for a man. Geometrics, which are hard to find, can be a welcome addition to all our quilts, and help to keep them from becoming "cutesy." They provide another way of getting contrast. (See Figure 1.11.)

Stripes, another overlooked division, may be composed of solid lines in equal or varying widths, employing one or more than one color. As yardage, they may have a very humble appearance but they have the potential for adding a great deal of interest to our quilts. They can serve as an interesting foil for floral prints and can also give a feeling of movement (Figure 1.12).

Some stripes are actually composed of design elements lined up to create the feeling of a narrow solid line. I call these border stripes (Figure 1.13).

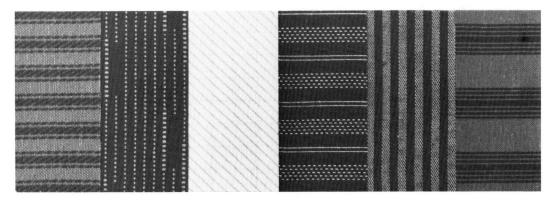

Figure 1.12

Figure 1.13

Narrow border stripes can be used like regular stripes or they can be sewn onto another fabric which is then used to outline individual shapes within a block or areas within a quilt (Figure 1.14).

Narrow border stripes can also be combined with other fabrics, for example a repeat, in a series of combinations to compose a unique border that can be used to surround an entire area (Figure 1.15).

Wide border prints, many specifically designed for inclusion in quilts (especially medallion quilts) can also be used for borders. Quite a few variations appear within one width, with the variations repeated regularly. Check the number of repeats to calculate the yardage required to border all sides of your quilt. Each time you add an additional border, select another variation to make maximum use of your fabric. Consider combining borders from different prints to cut down on the chance of someone else accidentally duplicating your quilt (Figure 1.16).

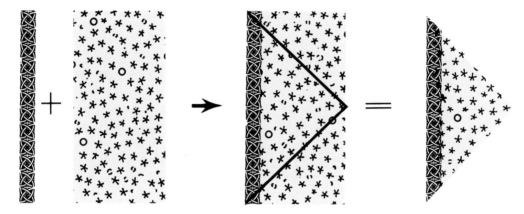

Figure 1.14

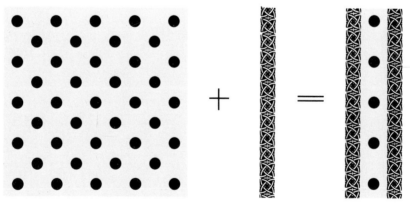

Figure 1.15

Figure 1.16

Plaids are found with great frequency in antique quilts but are seldom considered by today's average quiltmaker. Because many quilters come from a sewing background, they are overly concerned about keeping fabric on grain, since plaids and stripes readily show if they are off grain. Many of us therefore don't use these directional patterned fabrics because too much time is required to keep them exactly on grain. Once again we're missing a golden opportunity for some creativity in our quilts. More about this in the next lesson. Suffice it to say that, in general, plaids can provide welcome relief from too much calico (Figure 1.17). Add them to your collection!

Figure 1.17

The final division under design layout is "wonder prints," a catch-all term for fabrics which don't fall neatly and tidily into any category. Wonder prints can be looked at in two ways—as in "I wonder what this will be?" or as in "Look at all the things this can be."

Let's deal with the second thought first as it's the easiest to describe. Some prints are composed of areas of different designs contained within one piece of yardage. Sometimes they are built almost like a crazy quilt. Depending where you cut, you get different things. Often hard to find designs are contained on this type of fabric—for example, geometrics or linear-type designs. I buy these fabrics as I see them and figure out later how they will be used. (See Figure 1.18.)

Figure 1.18

Fabrics that fit the question "I wonder what this will be?" require the most imagination. One of my favorite examples is a piece of fabric in my collection that contains a large drawing of a chimpanzee. The fabric is very ugly to everyone but my daughter, who adores animals. When you ignore the picture itself and examine the surface just for the designs, you discover wonderful shapes and textures in the print. For example, the fur could be dirt in a farm scene (Figure 1.19).

Figure 1.19

Wonder prints, then, don't look like traditional calico prints. I follow my standard requirements about correct weight and fiber content, although occasionally I find a piece that I must have that doesn't comply. I let my imagination run wild. I call this process visualizing in fabric. This type of yardage will probably not be carried at your local quilt shop. Many towns have a store that seems to specialize in unusual, often peculiar or even ugly fabric. Sometimes you'll find this fabric in a discount mart or perhaps on the big sale table at the back of your general yardage store. Don't neglect exclusive specialty yardage stores either. You only need small pieces of wonder prints to add that special touch. One aid is to use a white card into which you have cut a 2″ window in the middle. Now move the card over the fabric to locate the intriguing areas. Viewing the print through this small opening is less distracting than seeing it as a large piece of yardage (Figure 1.20).

In summary, fabric can be looked at in many ways. Don't be afraid to branch out in your buying and to add some stimulating selections to your collection. The fabric itself can be the stimulus for making a quilt. Just looking at my fabric collection makes me feel creative.

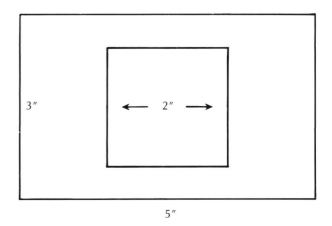

Figure 1.20

Figure 1.21.   World Without End. 66" × 80". Martha Currance, Missouri, 1900. Collection of author.

2

Learning to Use Patterned Fabric

Being able to see patterned fabric in different ways is the first step in learning how to work with it. Now you're ready to do some experimenting. Our goal is to make the viewer get caught up in our quilts, and an interesting use of patterned fabric will help us reach this goal. The viewer should become fascinated and feel drawn to our work. What a nice compliment when someone says, "I can't keep my eyes off your quilt!"

The following exercises have been designed to help you make some comparisons and then draw some conclusions. You will learn the most if you physically participate in these exercises. Space has been provided for your own glued mock-ups. A glue stick (shaped like a lipstick tube and available at quilt, grocery, and stationery stores) seems to work the best for attaching patterned fabric swatches to the paper. Wet glues can discolor the fabric or form distracting spots. Treat this book like a workbook. Really use it!

Illustration by Lisa Krieshok

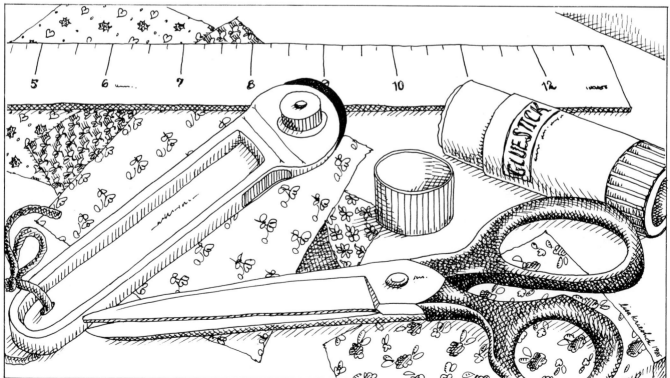

Figure 2.1

Value

Value refers to the lightness or darkness of your fabric. Value contrast establishes the pattern in a quilt block. Some quilt patterns have the potential to be read as different designs, merely by changing the placement of the dark, medium, and light values within that block.

Let's work with a typical quilt pattern, the Eight Pointed Star. Each star requires three pieces of fabric, representing dark, medium, and light values (see Figure 2.1):

      dark value = points of the star
  medium value = center square
    light value = background

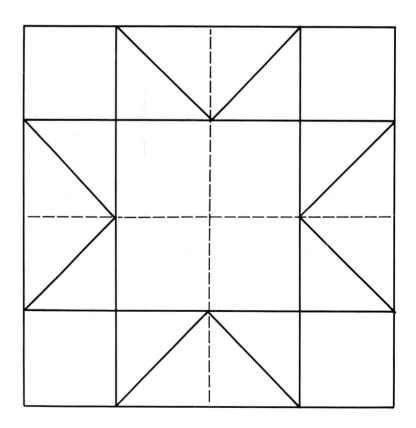

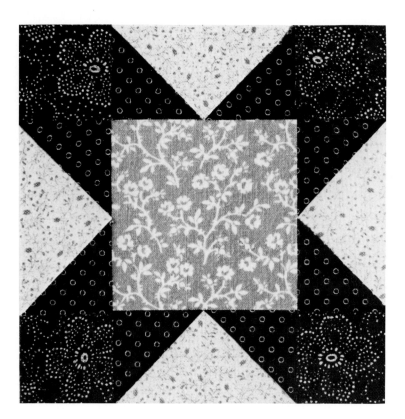

Figure 2.2A

To the original three fabrics, add a new one which is also a dark value. The color of the addition can be the same or different from the original dark fabric. The more closely the two match in regards to hue and value, the more they will read as the same fabric, except on close inspection. The new fabric can be placed in two different areas, either the corner squares or the perimeter triangles. Each new arrangement reads as a different pattern from the original star because your eyes add together all the dark areas to create a new shape. Keep the light fabric as the background and the medium as the center (Figure 2.2 A and B).

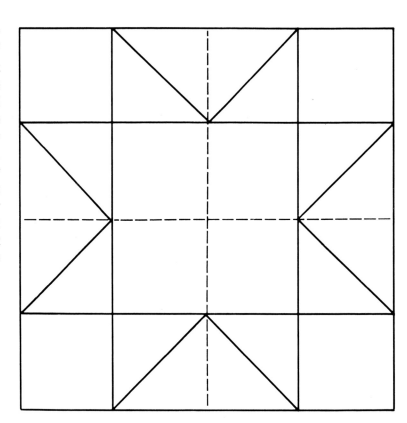

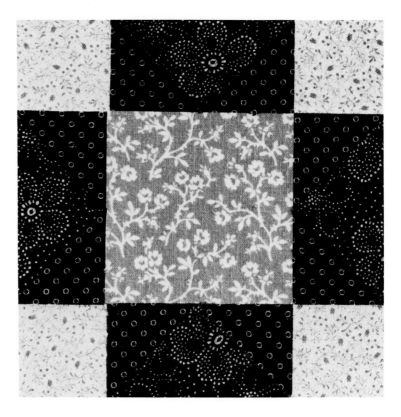

Figure 2.2B

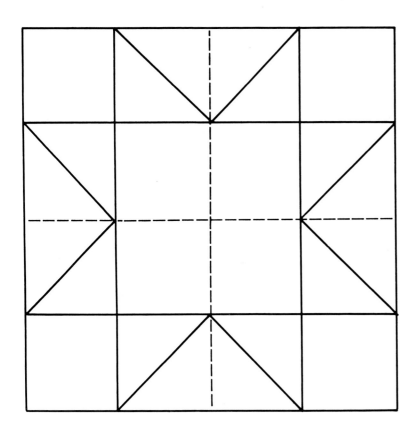

Figure 2.3A

Or instead, try adding a medium value fabric, this time of a different hue, to the original combination. Keep the center and the background the same as in Figure 2.1. It's possible to create an optical illusion of three-dimensionality in the version with the medium value in the corner squares. Your eyes no longer read that star as an X; instead it feels more cube-like on the ends, as in a baby's block pattern. Remember that different values are read as being on different visual planes (Figure 2.3 A and B).

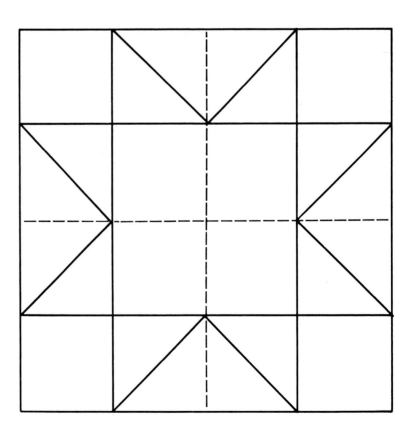

Figure 2.3B

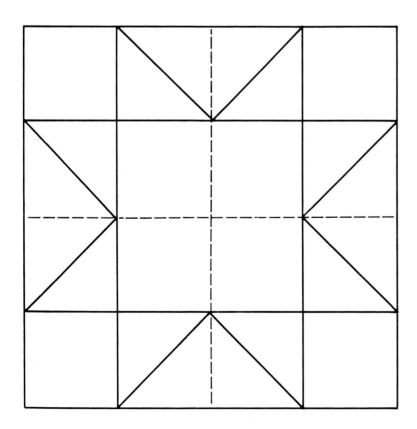

Five different blocks or variations have been created from one quilt pattern just by rearranging the value placement within the block. This is one way to add interest to your quilt. It's not necessary for all blocks within a repeat block quilt to read exactly the same way. This accidentally happens when you start adding new selections to replace your original fabrics if you happen to run out while making a quilt. Have you noticed that our quilts are almost always more interesting and exciting when we miscalculate yardage and are forced to make substitutions to complete the quilt? This is partly why scrap quilts work so well.

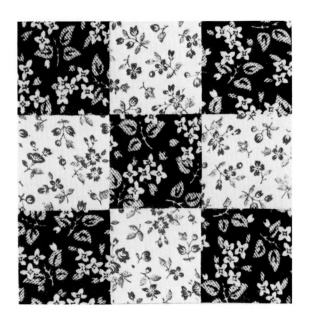

Figure 2.4A Small + Small

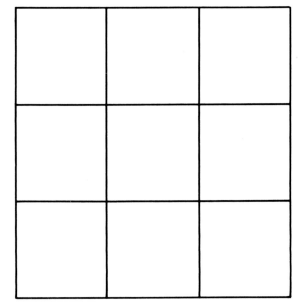

Figure 2.4B Large + Large

Scale

Scale refers to the size of the pattern on the fabric. Scale change within our fabric selection provides us the opportunity to create some viewer interest. Let's work with a nine-patch block. Consider the size of the prints when you make your choices, making one a light value and one a dark value. Try to make the selections as identical in scale as possible for each exercise.

This time we will work with three variations. In the first nine-patch, all the prints should be small scale (average calico). In the second nine-patch, the two fabrics should be large scale (bigger than typical calico). For the final variation, combine some small-scale fabric from the first block with some of the large-scale fabric from the second block (Figure 2.4 A, B and C).

Figure 2.4C Small + Large

Now study these blocks and consider the following questions:

- Which block looks the most like a traditional quilt block?_____

- Which block looks the least interesting? _____

- Does one block look too busy?_____

- Is one block more exciting than the others?
  _____

- Which block keeps your interest the longest?
  _____

The small-scale block looks the most like a traditional quilt block but is usually more static than the others. The large-scale block can look very exciting or be too busy, depending on the selection of fabrics used. You may want to do some more experimenting with using large-scale fabric. The small- plus large-scale block has the most chance of being the best looking, because of the interesting variations for our eyes to take in. If everything is too similar, your eyes won't spend the time to examine each part; they will just skim over the whole. Remember the idea is to keep the viewers' attention; you can accomplish this by making their eyes linger on the fabric.

Centering a Print

It's possible to take some repeat prints and position the template for cutting so that the design itself appears in the middle of each shape. Select two repeat prints; include a dark and a light value. Make two nine-patches from this fabric. When cutting the fabric for the first version, make sure that the fabric motif is centered or arranged so the motifs are identically placed as to position each time that fabric appears in the block. (See Figure 2.5).

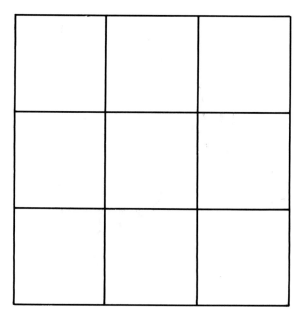

Figure 2.5　Centered Prints

When making the second version, cut the fabrics in the traditional quiltmaking approach, conserving and making maximum use of the fabric. This time the motifs will be positioned in a random manner (Figure 2.6).

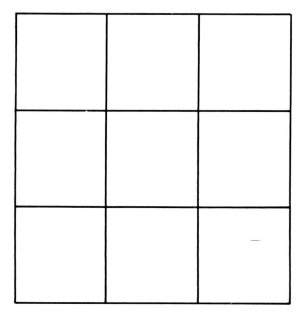

Figure 2.6　Random Prints

Lesson 2 continues after color section.

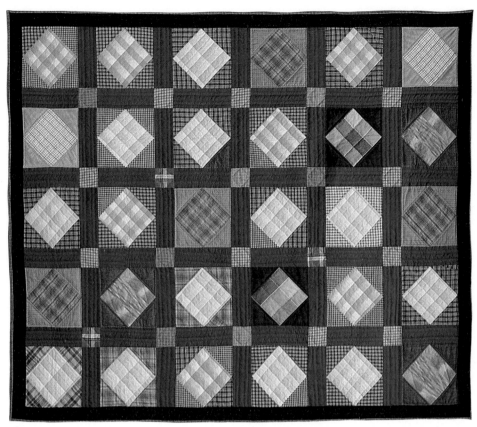

A

1

A   *Homespun Diamond In A
Square*
71″ x 61″
Roberta Horton
pieced and quilted by
Roberta Horton and
Mary Mashuta
Berkeley, CA   1985

B   *My Scrappy Delight*
31″ x 31″
Janet Shore
El Cerrito, CA   1985

B

A

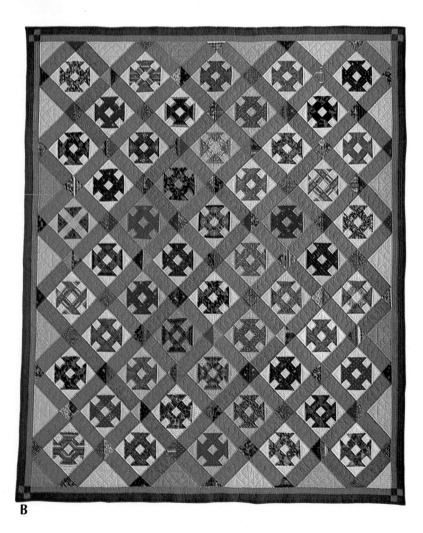

2

A *Pieced and Patched Stars*
49″ x 58″
Roberta Horton
pieced and quilted by
Roberta Horton and
Mary Mashuta
Berkeley, CA   1985

B *Churn Dash*
90″ x 108″
Setsuko Shimizu
San Leandro, CA   1984

B

A

3

A *Mail Pouch*
95″ x 60″
Cathie Hoover
Modesto, CA   1985

B *Old Maid's Puzzle*
74″ x 94″
Connie Kossa
Berkeley, CA   1985

B

4

A *Garden Patch*
42″ x 42″
Judy Kronmiller
Lafayette, CA   1985

B *Mendocino* (front)
C *Mendocino* (back)
51″ x 59″
Gay Nichols
Albany, CA   1985

A

B

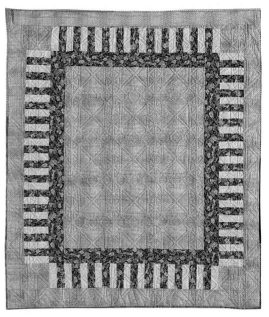

C

A

5

A   *Kaleidoscope*
    59" x 52"
    Gai Perry
    Walnut Creek, CA   1985

B   *Cube Lattice In Neon*
    39" x 32"
    Nancy Taylor
    Pleasanton, CA   1985

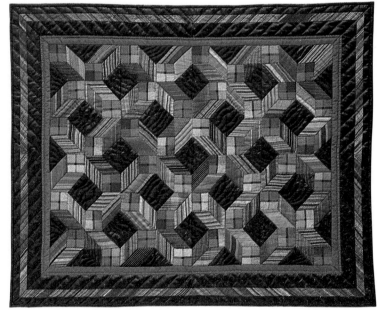

B

A

B

6

A *Shades of Japan*
27″ x 33″
Sue Arnold
Albany, CA   1982

B *Summer Day*
28″ x 29″
[Sashiko Quilting]
Connie Kossa
Berkeley, CA   1985

C *Dunn's Window*
38″ x 42″
Roberta Horton
quilted by
Roberta Horton and
Mary Mashuta
Berkeley, CA   1982

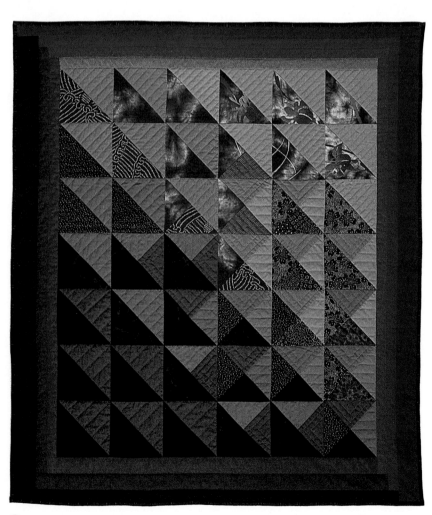

C

A

B

C

7

A *Butterflies Are Free*
45″ x 45″
Janet Hellerich
Richmond, CA   1985

B *The Swimmer*
23″ x 35″
Betty Kaspin
Richmond, CA   1985

C *Emerging Diamonds*
21″ x 58″
Joy Firtell
Moraga, CA   1985

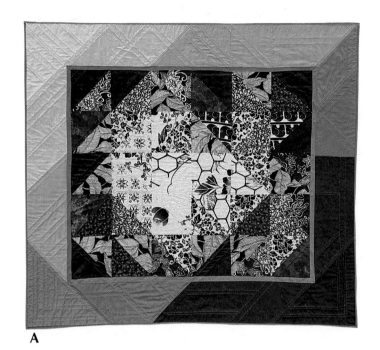

A

B

C

8

A   *Moon Over Hakone*
46″ x 42″
Celia LoPinto
San Francisco, CA   1984

B   *Yamanaka* ('Amidst the
Mountains')
28″ x 37″
Kay Starkweather
El Cerrito, CA   1983

C   *Winged Undercurrents*
43″ x 50″
Roberta Horton
quilted by
Roberta Horton and
Mary Mashuta
Berkeley, CA   1982

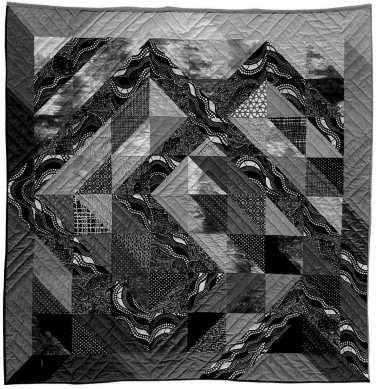

A

9
───────────────

A *Tsunami* ('Tidal Wave')
50" x 49"
Susan Dahlgren
Lafayette, CA   1985

B *Dancing Nine-patches*
18" x 66"
Cynthia Horton
(age 13½)
quilted by
Adelaide Mashuta and
Roberta Horton
Berkeley, CA   1984

B

A

10

A *Kyoto*
49″ x 51″
Miriam Nathan-Roberts
Berkeley, CA
quilted by Lizzi Kurtz
Charm, Ohio   1982

B *Angle of Repose*
50″ x 62″
Gay Nichols
Albany, CA   1983

C *Star Stuff*
42″ x 64″
Laurel Samberg DeBiasi
Lafayette, CA   1985

B

C

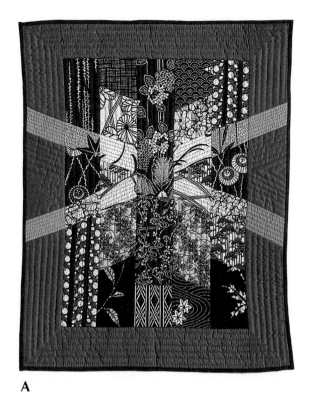

A

B

11

A *X Marks the Spot!*
23″ x 29″
Elizabeth Stypes
Walnut Creek, CA   1985

B *Go Tai Hachi* ('5 to 8')
38″ x 59″
Jane Richardson
Mill Valley, CA   1985

A

B

12

A *Foggy Day Leaves*
34" x 43"
[Sashiko Quilting]
Roberta Horton
quilted by
Roberta Horton and
Mary Mashuta
Berkeley, CA   1983

B *Tahoe Dreamin'*
30" x 40"
Judy Mullen
Manteca, CA   1983

C *My Japanese Quilt*
37" x 43"
Barbara Weirick
Orinda, CA   1985

C

A

B

13

A *Twirling Baskets*
   44″ x 44″
   Mary Schoenfeldt
   Berkeley, CA   1984
   Collection of Author

B *Secret Garden*
   46″ x 58″
   Gay Nichols
   Albany, CA   1984

A

14

A *Effie's Quilt*
41″ x 29″
Gai Perry
Walnut Creek, CA   1985

B *Beezaar*
49″ x 45″
Cathie Hoover
Modesto, CA   1985

B

A

B

C

15

A   *Shooting Stars* (front)
B   *Shooting Stars* (back)
    26" x 34"
    Mary Schoenfeldt
    Berkeley, CA   1984

C   *Jubilation*
    33" x 32"
    Gay Nichols
    Albany, CA   1984

A

16

A *Cajun Baskets*
51″ x 64″
Laurel Samberg DeBiasi
Lafayette, CA   1985

B *Houses*
41″ x 41″
Mabry Benson
quilted by
Mabry Benson and
Five Easy Piecers
Kensington, CA   1985

B

Study the variations and then consider the following questions:

- Which nine-patch took the longest to cut?

  ———

- Which nine-patch is the most controlled or static?

  ———

- Which nine-patch seems to have the most vitality?

  ———

Centering a print takes a lot of fabric and time. Imagine doing this for an entire quilt! This is one of the ways I feel we are overworking our quilts today. Quiltmakers during pioneer times did not have the time or fabric to follow this practice. There is a vitality in their scrap quilts which we can envy. Maybe what they did out of necessity is the best approach after all.

Directional Fabric

Directional patterned fabrics feature stripes or plaids. Antique quilts abound with them, yet they seem to be forgotten by the average quiltmaker of today. Actually this category of fabric can do a great deal for our quilts if we understand how to use them.

Grainline is very obvious in directional fabrics. The true grain of the fabric is represented by a line parallel or perpendicular to the selvage (Figure 2.7). If the fabric is a woven design, then the threads which create the pattern represent the grain. If the directional design is created through printing, you have a choice of what to do about the grainline. You can use the true grain, which might not line up with the printed lines, or you can use the printed lines and ignore the true grain if there's a difference. Quiltmakers from a sewing background tend to be very rigid about the importance of grainline. Consider that when small pieces are used, grainline isn't as crucial as when you're cutting out a garment where its final hang is important. When making your decisions about what to do with grain in directional prints, use the obvious printed one.

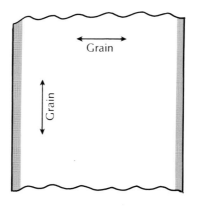

Figure 2.7

We will make two more nine-patches for comparison. Select two directional prints or weaves, remembering to include a dark and a light value. Arrange all the fabrics on grain in the first example. Reuse the fabrics in the same place for the second example, this time making all the pieces off grain. Don't have the individual pieces cut from one fabric repeat the identical degree of being off grain. Be more random. (See Figure 2.8 A and B.).

 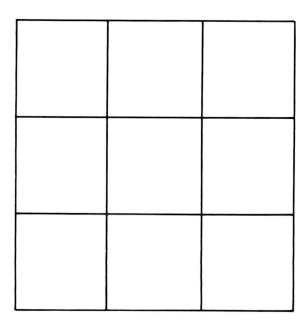

Figure 2.8A   On-Grain

 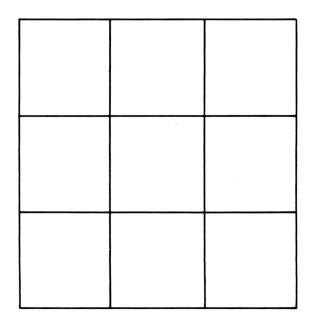

Figure 2.8B   Off-Grain

Now compare the two examples:

- Which nine-patch is the most static?_____

- Which nine-patch shows the most movement?

  _____

- Which nine-patch is the most exciting?_____

The on-grain nine-patch is very predictable in comparison to the off-grain nine-patch. The off-grain nine-patch shows movement, perhaps too much for your tastes. We can see graphically how to create or suggest movement through fabric selection.

Let's make one change to the on-grain nine-patch. Select one of the directional fabrics and patch it with matching fabric somewhere within the block. Experiment until you discover the best looking patch. Don't be tempted to exactly match your patch with the existing grain and don't try to make your patch perfectly chevron with the existing fabric. You'll find that the "worst" match is often the most artistic (Figure 2.9).

I hope these exercises provide new insights into using printed and patterned fabrics in your quilts. The remainder of the book will take what you've learned and put it to practical application.

Figure 2.9

3

Scrap Quilts

Quite simply, one of the reasons I am interested in quilts is the fabric in them. Old quilts contain such interesting prints, plaids, and stripes. Looking at the selection of fabrics in a quilt shows what one quilter had available at a given time. Some quilts are obviously planned because the fabric is repeated consistently throughout. The quilts that I find the most intriguing, however, are the ones made from a wide variety of fabrics, what we refer to here as scrap quilts. Part of their appeal is that very variety; sometimes, in fact, a particular print will only appear in one place in a quilt (Figure 3.1).

Figure 3.1. Medallion scrap quilt (top). 1850. Collection of author.

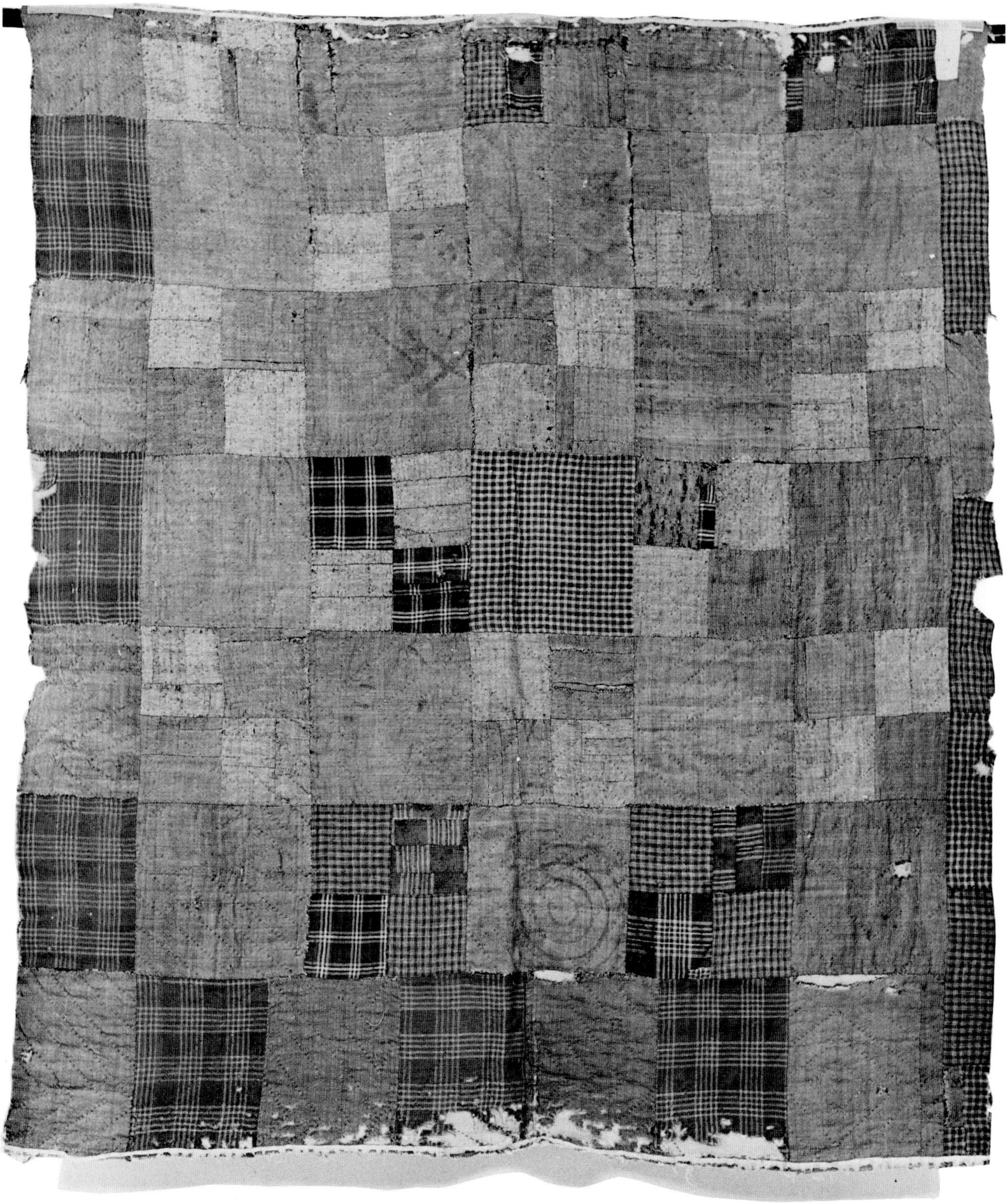

Figure 3.2A. Pieced quilt, woolen; four-patch block from Collingwood, Nova Scotia. Supposed to be c. 1810. Courtesy Nova Scotia Museum, Halifax, Canada.

Some people are under the mistaken assumption that all quilts are or were made using scrap fabric. This romantic notion overlooks that there's no way to document how fabric was amassed for a quilt. For the purpose of this book, we will consider a scrap quilt to be one composed of many different fabrics used in a *random* fashion. It's not enough that many fabrics are used. If the fabrics have been controlled to the extent that a particular fabric consistently appears in the same place in all the blocks, I don't consider it a scrap quilt. It also doesn't really matter if the fabric is left-over from other sewing projects or whether it's newly purchased with a particular quilt in mind. The hallmarks of a scrap quilt are the use of many fabrics and the random use of fabric within the blocks.

One term often heard in reference to types of scrap quilts is a "charm quilt." A charm quilt is composed of fabrics which are only used once in the quilt. There are periodic fads for charm quilts. Part of the fun in making this type of quilt is in gathering all the different fabrics.

Another frequently heard term is "utility quilt." This is often used in a mildly derogatory way, as in "It's only a utility quilt." These quilts were most likely made from true scraps and were made to keep someone warm, with no glamour thrown in. They represent the humble beginnings of our "fancy" quilts. I find these quilts very appealing. They remind me of mutt dogs and alley cats in contrast to pedigreed show animals. They have a particular charm and vitality all their own.

Homespun Quilt Project

This first exercise is intended to set the mood, to get you back to the beginning. If it helps, imagine yourself in a log cabin in the woods.

Many of the early utility quilts were made from a fabric called homespun, which looks like a heavy gingham. It was frequently woven at home, but was also commercially produced. Most of these quilts simply wore out; few have been saved by museums. Of those that remain, many showcase a sprightly combination of plaid patterns. The individual pieces are often pieced themselves, providing a wonderful texture to the surface. Study Figure 3.2 A and B.

Gather together as many small-scale plaids as you can find. In your quest, don't ignore the cuffs, pockets, or tails of worn-out plaid shirts belonging to family members.

Follow this recipe:

1. use a simple pattern
2. limit fabrics to plaids and stripes
3. both match and mismatch plaids within the blocks
4. make some plaids off grain
5. patch some areas (see Appendix)
6. quilt in a simple manner

The quilt in Photo 1A follows this formula. I made it as a tribute to the early homespun quilts I saw in several log cabin restorations. Initially I wondered why the maker had used the gingham-like fabric, as I thought it homely. (I had gotten my fill of plaids when I was in the eighth grade and pleated, plaid skirts were the vogue!) I was told that the plaids were homespun and were the only fabric available in that area at that time. What a thought! The quilter not only had to make the quilt but the fabric. Those quilts opened my mind and allowed me to appreciate what I consider to be the most humble origins of our traditional American quilts, those made by the common quilter.

Figure 3.2B. Detail, Figure 3.2A. Courtesy Nova Scotia Museum, Halifax, Canada.

Figure 3.3. *Birds In The Air* (detail). 72″ × 85″. Elkhart County, Indiana, 1880. Collection of author.

Scrap Quilt Project

Scrap quilts can be made from simple quilt block patterns. They don't require fancy, elaborate designs because the variety of fabric they contain is one of the main reasons they hold viewer interest. The quilt in Photo 1B contains only one shape. Manipulation of value helps to give the quilt an overall pattern. Or you may want to select a pattern which can be read in multiple ways because of the value changes within the blocks. Photos 2A and 5A are examples.

Many scrap quilts are repeat block quilts, meaning one pattern is duplicated over and over again. The use of fabric within a block tends to be consistent or uniform. The fabric in one block doesn't match the fabric in the next block. Interest can be added by turning the directional fabric different ways, placing some fabric off grain, or patching. These manipulations aren't done in every block. Some blocks should be simple and straightforward. (Figure 3.3)

The pattern blocks can be placed next to each other, as in Photo 3B. This sometimes allows bigger, more complicated shapes to be created. Or the blocks may be joined with alternate plain blocks, as in Photo 3A. The pieced blocks made from patterned fabric offer limited opportunity for elaborate quilting so these plain blocks present an area for some fancy work. The third alternative is sashing as in Photo 2B. Both the second and third choices are ways of enlarging the quilt. (See Appendix for joining information.)

Scrap quilts can also be composed of two patterns, used in a checkerboard fashion. Photo 4A and Figure 3.4 are examples of this approach.

Midwestern scrap quilts usually have no borders, just a binding. If a border is present, it tends to be quite simple, consisting of several fairly narrow strips of varying width. I like this frugal approach, as it complements the simplicity of the quilt.

I suggest trying to find wall space to pin up your work as it progresses. Many quilters lay their work out on the floor and then stand back and inspect it. The problem is that the fabrics and shapes closest to the viewer are the correct size, while those further away (at the top) are smaller. Being able to see the right answer has partly to do with things being in the right proportion to each other. I work on a wall covered with white felt. The fabric shapes adhere to the felt and are eventually pinned in place when the final arrangement is determined. (See Appendix.)

Figure 3.4.   16-Patch Pinwheels (detail). 91″ × 58″. Judy Mullen, Manteca, CA, 1985.

Here are two creative approaches to try when making a scrap quilt, after having selected the pattern and overall color scheme. Be sure to read the fabric explanation in Lesson 1 and do the exercises in Lesson 2 before selecting the fabric. Those exercises are intended to stretch your mind about fabric usage and your mind should be in the "altered" state before you proceed.

Option A

As in a traditional quiltmaking approach, make some blocks by determining the fabric selection for each one, and then construct the individual blocks. At this point, you don't know the required number because the set will help to determine the number that will give you the desired size. You don't have to know in advance which set you will use. Leave yourself open for options and let the quilt help you make that decision. When you have a fair number of blocks made, try the following:

1. Arrange the blocks so the edges would be parallel to the edge of the quilt. Now place the blocks on point. Compare. Sometimes a block is much more interesting on point because its construction isn't so obvious. (See Figure 3.5.)

2. Now experiment with the set. Try adjacent blocks, alternate blocks, and sashing. Try different joining colors until you find the one that does the most for the fabrics already used. You may be surprised with the solution to both color and set. If you choose to use sashing, a medium or dark color will probably do the most to pull the blocks together. If you choose to set with alternate plain blocks, you might want to opt for a light or medium color so that fancy quilting will show well.

3. After selecting the set, make enough additional blocks to get the quilt to the correct size. Join the blocks.

4. Pin the completed top up on the wall and consider how you might border it.

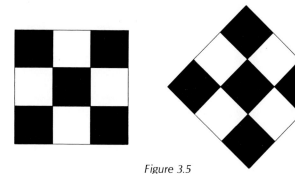

Figure 3.5

Option B

Decide upon the pattern size and set based on the dimensions you would like the quilt to be. Divide the possible fabrics into piles according to how they might be used. When I made the quilt in Photo 2A, I wanted dark value prints for the points of the stars; for the centers I wanted medium value, large-scale, or directional patterns; for the background I wanted light value, low contrast fabrics. Here was my recipe:

1. the completed quilt will look antique
2. the pattern block can be read several ways
3. each fabric will only appear in one block
4. some areas will be patched like old quilts

I knew there would be six rows of five blocks each. I started with the star points. Working from the appropriate pile, I began cutting out the points and placing them on the felt in their approximate position until I had the beginnings of thirty blocks. I worked in order on the stars, each time looking through my pile until I found a fabric I wanted to use.

Next I moved to the medium value pile. As I picked up each selection, I determined where I felt it would look the best. So this time, I didn't fill in the stars in order. When each center piece was cut, I could audition it in many places until I felt that I had found the best place for it. I had to start paying attention to what was already positioned in making that decision.

Finally, I began to work with the background pile. As I picked up each piece, I moved it around until I found it a home. I had to decide which blocks should read as crosses and which as X's so I could add in the appropriate value fabric to make that happen. Again, I didn't work on the blocks in order. The blocks aren't sewn until the quilt is completely composed.

Now, let's contrast the two methods. In Option A, the blocks are made independently of each other; then their order and set is determined. The quilt itself helps you to make many important decisions about its final appearance. In Option B, the set and number of blocks is predetermined. The blocks are composed in their ultimate position in the quilt. One limitation to this approach is that you can't suddenly decide to make the quilt bigger; you have balanced things as

you've gone along and you're locked into the placement of each block. It's fun to work this way, however, and you'll find yourself putting fabrics and designs into a block you previously wouldn't have chosen to combine because you can see how each possibility looks with the adjacent blocks.

The traditional approach of building one block at a time, as if creating a pillow, can make the quiltmaker overly concerned with the appearance of each block. The tendency is to make the block "pretty." When you study antique scrap quilts, you'll discover some downright "ugly" blocks in them, ones that would be awful as a pillow, yet that make the quilt work, that give it character and life. The ugly blocks even make the pretty blocks look better. Work on at least four blocks simultaneously if you use Option A; fabric choice decisions can be made much faster because each piece of fabric doesn't seem as important. And you'll be able to see how it helps to have one of the blocks ugly.

Neither of these options has employed the use of graph paper. Modern quiltmakers often plan their quilt design on graph paper, using colored pencils to indicate color choices. I find the usefulness of this method limited. First, the color of the pencils is never the same as the fabric. Second, the colored pencils can't possibly represent the complexity of patterned fabric. If you want to sketch out the quilt in advance on graph paper, work just with the idea of dark, medium, and light values indicated with black, grey, and white pencils. Then start composing with the real fabric on your felt.

Doing a glued mock-up with actual fabric can be far more helpful than using colored pencils and graph paper, but the temptation is to work out one portion of the quilt and then predictably repeat that solution for the rest of the quilt. Remember, according to the definition of a scrap quilt as used here, the fabric should appear in a random fashion. This would require you to mock-up the entire quilt. I prefer to work "live in the fabric" where there's the opportunity for spontaneity. It's such a joyful experience and not as wasteful of fabric as you might think. When you audition fabric candidates, if they don't fit in one place, save them to recycle into another spot.

4

Working with Nontraditional Fabric (Japanese Patchwork)

Calico is the most common type of fabric used in modern quilts. In Lessons 1 and 2, I have tried to broaden the possible choices beyond the ubiquitous calico. When I tired of calicoes, I began experimenting with other fabrics and found their use both scary and exciting.

Because I live in San Francisco Bay Area, with its large Asian population, one of the fabrics available to me is Japanese Yukata. Yukata is 14" wide, made from cotton, and a popular fabric for summer kimonos. Designs are either female or male; female patterns are generally floral while male designs tend to be geometric or linear. The most widely used color scheme is indigo blue and white although other colors appear. The printing or dyeing of the true Yukata goes through the fabric so that it's reversible; this handy feature means you can use either side. Yukata made specifically for export is only printed on one side, however. The fabric is also expensive in comparison to our calico, considering that it's much narrower.

I found this fabric exciting to look at and yet I couldn't immediately get a handle on how to use it myself. After much experimentation, I developed some new approaches and began teaching a class in 1982 on "Working With Nontraditional Fabrics." Eventually the class name evolved to "Japanese Patchwork" because we were working mostly with the Yukata. As always, I learned a tremendous amount from my students as we jointly tackled the problems this unique fabric presents. (Incidentally, we were working independently of what was happening in the quilting world in Japan, where the major focus at that time was in making ethnic–American quilts!)

The exercises in this lesson developed from my work with Japanese fabric, something at first alien to me. What I discovered was how to design a quilt where the fabric itself suggested the solution. I also began to better understand original design as seen in contemporary quilts. Finally, I ultimately came to understand

Figure 4.1. *Dragonfly.* [Sashiko Quilting] 32" × 40". Lydia McCowen, Walnut Creek, CA, 1984.

and better appreciate traditional American quilts, which led to my work with scrap quilts.

The book *Drawing on the Right Side of the Brain,* by Betty Edwards, addresses itself to the creative state I would like you to experience when working on the following exercises. I found Edwards' approach to creativity mirrored my own and my students' reactions to the class on nontraditional fabrics and to these exercises.

Basically, most of us are ruled by our left brain, which is dominant over the right brain. The brain processes information and comes to different conclusions depending on which brain hemisphere is doing the thinking. The left brain analyzes, counts, marks time, plans step-by-step procedures, verbalizes, and makes rational statements. The right brain relies on intuition and insight and is inventive and creative. It's considered the artistic side. Using the left brain, you figure things out in a logical order. When using the right brain, everything seems to just fall into place; in other words, you "get the picture." You can't say how you came to the conclusion, just that you know it's right. When in this state, you're unaware of the passage of time and

are totally absorbed in your project. You feel at one with the project.

These exercises are, therefore, intended for quilters who are ready to go beyond beginning. I hope they will serve to open your mind and make you more creative. You don't have to work with Japanese Yukata. Gather together some large-scale prints, some plaids and stripes, some batiks if available—anything that feels out-of-the-ordinary to you. Calico can be used as well as some solids.

Exercise #1 WORKING WITH ONE SHAPE

The fabric is going to make this project. It's probably best to work within a fairly limited color range, perhaps even being monochromatic. Don't work with a lot of multicolor prints as they will prove too distracting and hard to handle. Consider varying the scale and value. Then go through the following procedure:

1. *Select a single geometric shape.*

The only restriction is that fabric cut from that shape can be sewn together into a quilt. By limiting the complexity of the quilt to one pattern shape, the interest will have to come from the fabric itself.

The following quilts are all made from the same right angle triangle: Photos 6A, 8A, and 8B, and Figures 4.1, 4.2, and 4.3. An elongated version of that triangle can be seen in Photos 6B and 7C.

Figure 4.2. Tama ('Jewel'). [Sashiko Quilting] 24″ × 32″. Janet Shore, El Cerrito, CA 1982.

Figure 4.3. Pinwheel. 33″ × 33″. Valerie Yeaton, Oakland, CA, 1985.

2. *Determine the size of the chosen shape that looks good for your fabric.*

To decide this, use several pieces of unlined white paper to draw the proposed shape in several sizes. Don't include seam allowance but rather work with the finished size. Cut along the lines so that a window appears in each paper. For example, you might draw a 3", 4", and 5" version. (See Figure 4.4.)

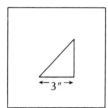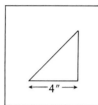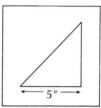

Figure 4.4

Move the windows over your fabric collection, trying to decide which size "feels" best. Does the smallest size seem to compress or squeeze the design on the fabric? Does the largest shape show too much of the fabric, making the design feel lost? You may have to cut other size trial shapes until you discover the size which feels best. It helps to think in terms of what is too small and what is too large. If you can establish these two limits, the correct answer will be somewhere in between. (See Figure 4.5.) I find that

Figure 4.5

large-scale prints look better in the larger sizes. Calico feels fine in the smaller sizes, but gets lost in the large shapes.

3. *Cut out fabric shapes in chosen size.*

Use your window template to identify "good" cuts. Move the window around the fabric until it captures a pleasing composition. Purposely don't center motifs. See if they are more interesting with only partial display of the design. Some prints look the same no matter where you cut.

Add on seam allowance before making your template for cutting. Cut out fabric shapes in a sufficient quantity to give you something with which to work. You will cut more as the work progresses.

4. *Arrange pieces in a composition on the wall.*

Work on a design wall (see Appendix). Try to get lost in the process; just do what feels good.

Start out simply. Experiment with possible arrangements. It's easiest to start thinking in terms of rows, with the same fabric being used throughout that row. This gives a sense of continuity. The row can be horizontal, vertical, or diagonal. Now add some more rows. To add interest, feature a different fabric in each row. See Photo 6A. Don't limit yourself only to florals; be sure to try some plaids and stripes.

Value changes can add interest, so think of your piece going from dark to light in a progression as in Photo 6A. Or reverse the order. Or try having it go from dark to light back to dark again as in Figure 4.6.

Try a random arrangement of value as in Photos 8A and 8B. Another possibility is off-setting the rows. You can even subdivide some of the pieces, as in Photos 6C and 7B.

Try and fill in an area that represents the finished perimeter with fabric pieces. One dimension should feel better to you. Rectangles are usually more interesting than squares; sometimes a long skinny shape is exciting.

5. *Critique the results.*

Now go back and critique what you *see*. A reducing glass is very helpful because the work will feel like someone else's when seen small (and it's always easier to give advice to another person than it is to see what your own work needs). Or take a picture of the quilt with an instant camera so you can see the results right away. The photo will give you a fresh view and problem areas are likely to show up that you hadn't noticed.

At this point your quilt may seem too simple and you may want to make some changes. Perhaps you need a spot of color to spark the piece (Photo 8B). Perhaps you need to turn one directional print a contrary way within one row (Figure 4.1). It's better to have the solution overly simple and then spice it up as opposed to trying to make too many things happen from the beginning.

As you work on the solution, try to be very right-brained; get lost in the project. This may have already happened to you as you've been working. If you have experienced a feeling of losing track of time, you've been using your right brain. If you can get to that place, you will "feel" when the right answer presents itself.

6. *Border the quilt.*

Borders can make a quilt. It's easier to border once the top has been sewn together. Now audition

Figure 4.6. Timothy's Fanfare. 39″ × 39″. Mary Madden ©, Topeka, KS, 1984.

the possibilities, remembering that the border can bring the whole piece together.

A simple border can be composed of one or two strips, as in Photo 7A. Pick up a color suggested in one of your fabrics. You can split the inner border into several colors, as in Photo 8A, or the outer border can be split into a variety of colors, keeping the inner border the same (Photo 6A). Or you can try splitting both the inner and outer borders, as in Photos 6B and 8A. You can also give a feeling of depth to your quilt by making it feel layered, as in Figures 4.1 and 4.2.

Option A: Log Cabin Project

This is a more advanced undertaking than the previous project. Play with the same rules, but this time see if you can make lines form in your quilt. I liken this to a log cabin quilt which is composed of squares diagonally divided into a light and dark side. As dark–light blocks are assembled, new overall patterns emerge. We can accomplish the same thing using half-of-a-square triangles with light and dark halves forming the square.

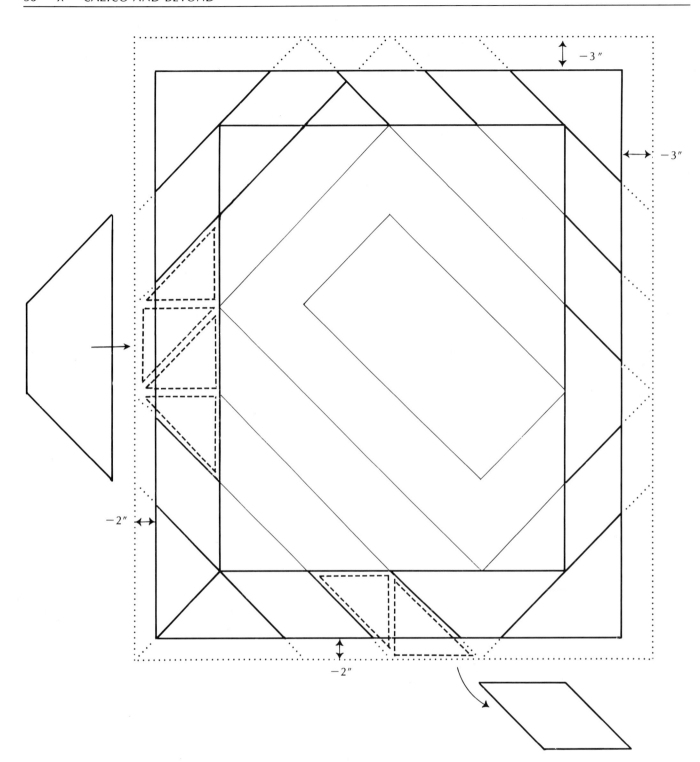

Figure 4.7

Study Photo 8C. You'll see that the shapes aren't as controlled and symmetrical as in a log cabin quilt. To help the abstract feeling, some of the lines go off the edge of the quilt, to re-enter at another place. That is, the whole design is not confined in the quilt. The total composition is also off-centered.

The border is really built on the idea of triangles, too. Where an area reads as one color, the triangles were added together and a new template was cut. The borders are also narrower than the width of the original triangle so its relationship is further obscured. In fact, the top and right border are more narrow than the bottom and left. (See Figure 4.7.)

Figure 4.8. Baby's Blocks.
30″ × 30″.
Yuri Uchiyama,
San Leandro, CA, 1982.

Option B: Dimension Project

Dimension is created through the use of different values which are then perceived to be on different visual planes. The Baby Blocks pattern in Figure 4.8 shows the consistent use of dark, medium, and light values to suggest that the blocks are truly dimensional. Now study Photo 10C in which the same pattern is used. Part of the time we can see the blocks but sometimes we see stars instead. Notice how the stars feel flat.

The quilt in Photo 10B uses triangles. Different shapes can be seen, depending on how the value was handled in a specific area. Also notice that your eyes keep moving through the design, focusing on one shape, then another.

Another pattern which can show dimension is Inner City. The basic shape is half a hexagon (Figure 4.9). There is a light and dark side, and those also can be

divided into upper lighter and lower darker, so that a total of four values can be used for each visual unit. Study Figures 4.10, 4.11, and 4.12, and Photo 10A for some different versions of the same pattern. Don't forget that humor can have a place in our quilts.

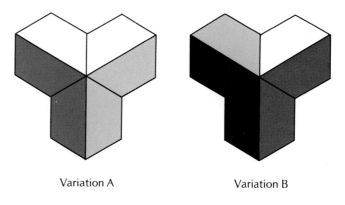

Variation A   Variation B

Figure 4.9

Figure 4.10.   San Francisco. [Sashiko Quilting] 37″ × 48″. Carol Schubb, Moraga, CA, 1985.

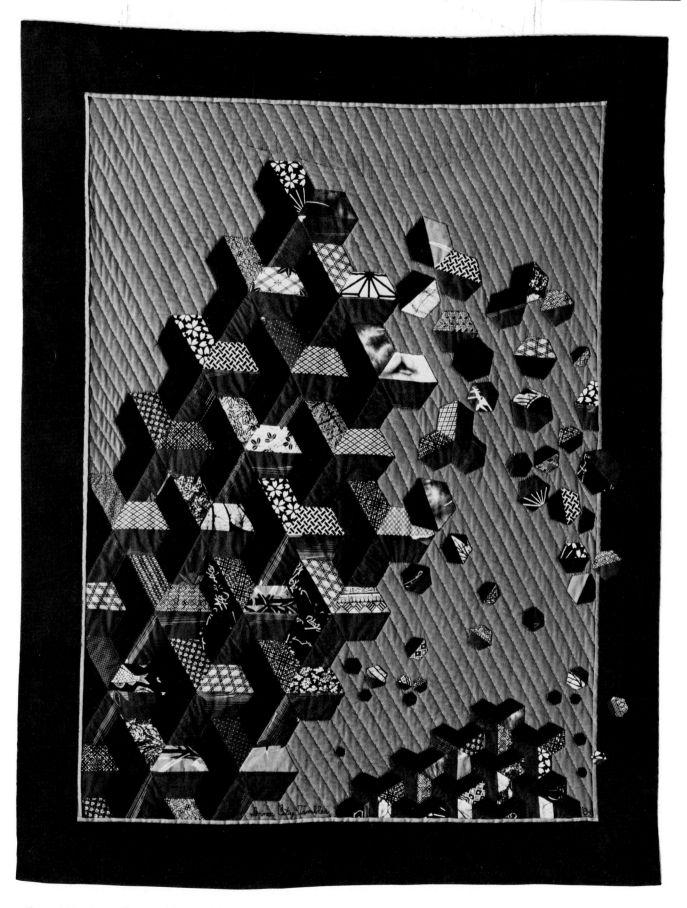

Figure 4.11. Inner City Tumbles. [Sashiko Quilting] 51" × 66". Helen Dyer, Seattle, WA, 1984.

Figure 4.12. Dokoisho. 43″ × 49″. Naoko Anne Ito, Berkeley, CA, 1984.

Exercise #2 WORKING IN ROWS

Now try working in another way, this time using your left brain and some graph paper to draw a quilt. Then you can switch over to your right brain and select the fabric to make the quilt itself. Proceed through the following steps:

1. *Make the quilt in rows.*

On graph paper draw the outline of the shape of the proposed quilt. Think in terms of later converting this drawing to an actual quilt, so have a given number of squares represent a particular measurement.

The quilt will be composed of rows which can be of identical width (Photo 11A) or variable width (Photos 12A and 12B). They can be horizontal or vertical. Draw some lines on the graph paper. Use a pencil so you can erase until you achieve a pleasing composition.

2. *Subdivide the rows into smaller units.*

The rows themselves now need to be broken down into smaller shapes by drawing lines perpendicular or diagonal to the original lines (Photo 11A). You may want to include some pieced blocks or strips (Photos 11B, 12A, and 12C). You may also want to leave some blank areas available for sashiko or quilting designs. (See Photos 11B and 12A.)

Study Figure 4.13, a representation of the original scale drawing for the quilt pictured in Photo 12A.

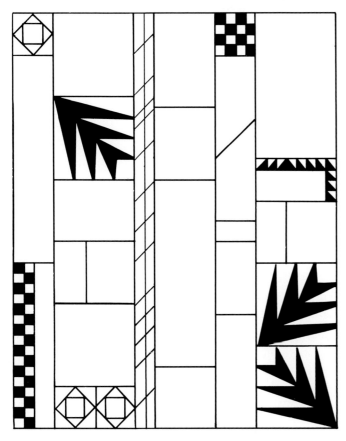

Figure 4.13

Notice that although some changes have been made in the execution, basically both the drawing and the quilt are alike.

3. *Audition fabric for the quilt.*

Work on the wall to build the quilt you have sketched. Cut template windows for each shape that requires a patterned fabric. Work through the shapes, filling in the fabric as you go. Keep in mind the need for light, medium, and dark areas. For the discipline, try and stay faithful to the original drawing as much as possible.

Exercise #3   **TRADITIONAL BLOCK**

Take the insights you have gained from the previous projects on using nontraditional fabrics and apply them to working with a traditional pieced block. Work on four blocks simultaneously. You may want to refer back to Lesson 3 on scrap quilts before proceeding. The quilts in Photos 13A and 13B are examples of this exercise.

5

Afro-American Quilts

Afro-American quilts offer a wonderful opportunity for the average quiltmaker to break out of the traditional quiltmaking mold and do some growing. I have found this to be true every time I've taught Afro-American quiltmaking. Students whose work and habits I am familiar with through previous classes have made major breakthroughs. They often enthuse about how exciting the design experience was; many of them have even made up elaborate fantasies to go along with their quilts. In fact, the fantasy often seemed necessary for that individual to break all the rules that had governed work up to that point. I consider the whole process very right brain.

Detailed information about Afro-American quilts has been slow to emerge.* Afro-American quilts are still being made in rural areas of the southern United States, mostly by elderly black women. They can be found in many black homes in urban areas but often aren't fully understood or appreciated by their current owners. The quilts may be treasured mainly because an ancestor or relative made them. Chances are if the present owner also quilts, she works in the Euro-American format. However, some blacks work in the Afro-American style without even realizing it because the quiltmaking customs have been passed on by example rather than by oral or written instructions. Afro-American cultural preferences are manifested throughout black society in many ways and can be seen in their music and art.

The design and structural elements differ between Euro-American and Afro-American quilts. Euro-American quilts stress repeat designs and symmetry. Small details of workmanship, such as having the

points match within a design, are important. Quilting stitches are admired for their smallness and regularity as well as for the element of design they add to the finished piece, although this seems more important in fancy than in utility quilts. Fabric coordination is considered pleasing when the selection matches or blends nicely and the result is harmonious or "pretty." These quilts are meant to be seen up close. Often many hours go into the construction of a quilt.

Afro-American quilts blend the design preferences of Africa with this American quilt tradition. The colors are bright and high contrast, with bold fabric patterns. Largeness of design, rather than smallness, is aimed for because the overall effect is more important than intricate details. The individual pieces or the blocks may be large scale because the quilts originally needed to be made quickly.

Rhythms are different for the two types of quilts. Euro-American quilts emphasize repetition and matching; Afro-American quilts stress improvisation and surprise, with multiple patterns being popular. The Euro-American design preference is for the grid format; the Afro-American quilt has a strong vertical feeling, possibly linked to the narrow woven textiles of Africa. There is also a marked preference for offsetting so that if a grid is used, chances are that the horizontal sashing units will not match up in each row. The quilt is constructed and viewed more as joined rows than as a checkerboard. (See Figure 5.1 and Figure 5.2.)

The strong folk-art feeling of many Afro-American quilts can confuse and confound people used to traditional American (really Euro-American) quilts. From

Figure 5.1. Strip Quilt. Martha Jane Pettway, Gee's Bend, AL. Photo supplied by Dr. Maude Southwell Wahlman ©. Photo by William Martin, Oxford, MS.

Figure 5.2. Cotton Leaf. Lucinda Toomer, 1890-1983, Dawson, GA. Photo courtesy of Dr. Maude Southwell Wahlman ©. Photo by William Martin, Oxford, MS.

a workmanship standpoint, Afro-American quilts, with their quality of "pinch and tuck" and "make do," have more in common with Euro-American utility quilts than with fancy quilts. Viewers may grant that the Afro-American quilts are exciting and colorful but the workmanship often doesn't quite live up to the usual standards of excellence. Remember these quilts originated during slave times when two of the necessary ingredients of Euro-American quilts, time and thread, were scarce. The quilts were necessary for survival to the slaves. Since they didn't have much free time for sewing, fast ways had to be found to make the quilts; hence, the use of large pieces and oversized patterns.

Spool thread was a rare commodity to rural blacks before the twentieth century. One source of thread was from feed and flour sacks which were unraveled. Big stitches used up less precious thread and time than did small stitches. So small and even quilting stitches never seemed to take on the importance, then, in Afro-American quilts that they did in Euro-American quilts. The quilting stitch used should be considered functional rather than decorative, that is, with just enough of them to hold the quilt layers together. The most common quilting designs used are concentric half circles, known as Baptist Fan or shells, as well as straight lines. The quilts in Photos 15A and 16B show the use of the fan motif, while the quilt in Photo 14B employs straight lines.

Probably one of the most misunderstood characteristics is the improvisation which is misread as doing the pattern incorrectly. Think about jazz and the black musicians who created this unique form of improvisational music. For Afro-American quilts, this same type of improvisation should be seen as positive and creative. The idea is to take one pattern and vary it, with changes in color or fabric use, value, scale, or in the actual construction of the block. Study Figure 5.3.

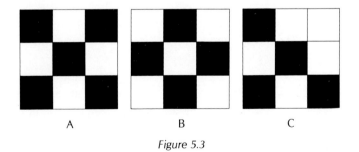

A   B   C

Figure 5.3

Versions A and B are two accepted variations frequently seen in Euro-American quilts, but version C is thought to be incorrect. Actually, it's just another variation. Think of the creative potential here! (Refer back to Figure 5.2.)

Working on Afro-American quilts can also represent an opportunity to add more fabric to your collection. High contrast, bold, wild fabrics can be used. Gather larger-scale prints than you normally use, multicolor prints . . . these can all be combined in ways you commonly wouldn't consider. Directional patterns are particularly good because of the visual movement they create. Often what feels appropriate in an Afro-American quilt is what you've previously rejected for quilt use. Study the quilt in Photo 16B. The lower left-hand block represents the most traditional use of fabric. The other three blocks are far more exciting and interesting. Notice how the fabric in the upper left corner is more important than the design itself, a fairly common characteristic of Afro-American quilts. The stripes in the house in the upper right make it feel as if it's about to tumble down.

The asymmetry in Afro-American quilts is created by the preference for off-setting. This can be seen in the assembly of the quilt blocks which are made into vertical rows but then not matched horizontally (see Photos 14B and 15C). Or it can happen within the block itself, which makes it seem fractured, and thereby more exciting (Photo 14B).

Afro-American Project

The major design characteristics of Afro-American quilts are:

1. vertical strip organization
2. bold color
3. large design elements
4. asymmetry
5. multiple patterning
6. improvised rhythm

Try and make a quilt using one, some, or all of these ideas. Not all characteristics appear in every Afro-American quilt. Incidentally, the finished quilt doesn't even have to conform to the usual standards of uniform borders or shape, one more exciting thought!

*The aesthetic principles mentioned in this lesson are courtesy of Dr. Maude Southwell Wahlman. The subject will be more fully explored in her book, *The Art of Afro-American Quiltmaking* (Bloomington: Indiana University Press. In Press.) My thanks to Dr. Wahlman for her invaluable help.

6

Quilt Backings and Bindings

Quilt backings have long intrigued me. When I became a quilter, I discovered that part of the correct protocol when viewing a quilt is to turn it over and inspect the back. One quilter is always very concerned with the quilting of another, and sometimes the stitching or the pattern show better on the back. Maybe the viewer will discover knots or something else that shouldn't be there. More positively, the viewer could be interested in the fabric the quiltmaker has chosen for her backing, since this tells a great deal about the maker.

Historically, fabric that was held in disfavor was often placed on the backside of a quilt. This can provide clues about attitudes and fashions prevalent during a given time period. For example, when store-bought fabric replaced homespun in availability, the homespun was relegated to the back. It was considered inferior to what could be purchased. The same can be said for hand-dyed fabric which is often found on the back of antique quilts. Today, we would proudly put the hand-dyed fabric on the front, being sure to mention its presence on the label or explanation in the quilt show program!

When viewing Depression era or rural quilts from this century, you'll sometimes find that the back is made from cloth flour or feed sacks that had first been bleached, then dyed. Two of my all-time favorite backings were composed of rice sacks and fertilizer bags, the words and logos still visible. The first quilt was made by a Japanese immigrant mail-order bride during the 1920s and the second by a poor black sharecropper living in the South during the Depression. Both of these backings make a historical statement.

As fashions changed, the popularity of certain kinds of fabric diminished. This out-of-favor fabric became a prime candidate for quilt backings. This practice continues to the present. A quilt store owner once told me she always backed her quilts with fabric that hadn't sold well in her store. This thrifty practice makes sense but doesn't sound like much fun. Such frugality is not necessarily artistically creative.

Many new quilters back their quilts with sheets because sheets are wide enough not to require seams. It wasn't until after 1800 that fabric was available in sufficient quantity to allow big pieces to be used for the backings, but even these had to be seamed since fabric wasn't woven as wide as quilts. So seams have always been present on the back. If you insist on using a sheet, choose a muslin over a percale, since the latter's high thread count makes it difficult to get the needle through the fabric when the quilting is done.

Quilt backings of yesteryear were often pieced out of necessity. Figure 6.1 shows the homespun used for the back of a nineteenth-century log cabin quilt. It was assembled in a quilt-as-you-go method, with the joining seams covered over with strips of homespun. Figure 6.2 shows the stripped backing of an antique Pennsylvania quilt. Note Photo 15B which depicts a typical pieced backing of an Afro-American quilt. I'm particularly fond of the fabric this contemporary quilter selected for her rod pocket, sewn across the top of the back of the quilt.

Occasionally, quilt backings were pieced for design reasons. As a quiltmaker, this is one of the options available to you. The back represents one more design surface. In Photo 4C, the backing suggests the

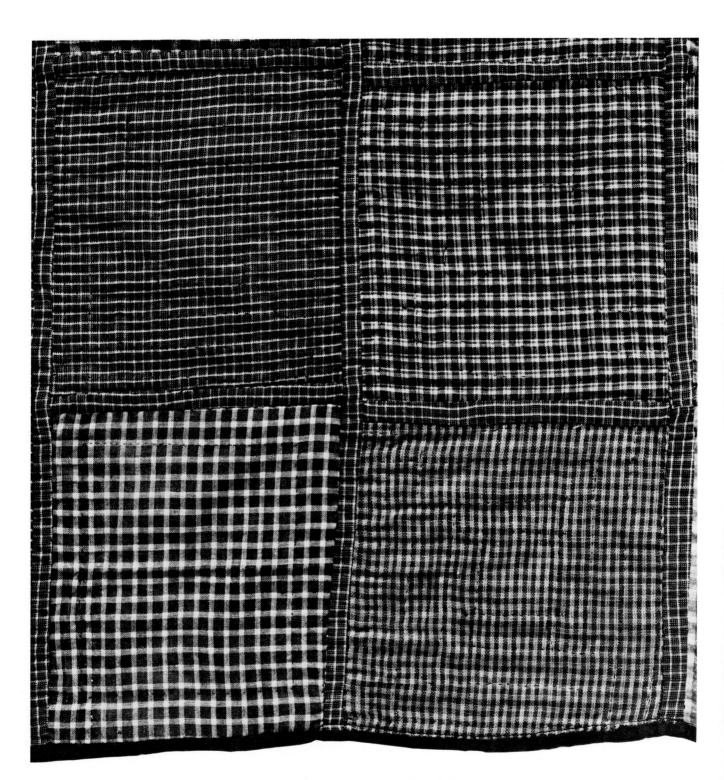

Figure 6.1.   *Log cabin* quilt (back detail). 61″ × 70″. Lancaster County, PA, 1870. Collection of author.

Figure 6.2. Frog In The Puddle (back). 60″ × 60″. Pennsylvania, 1910. Collection of author.

picket fences found in the quaint northern California coastal town of Mendocino, which also served as the inspiration for the coloration of the front of the quilt (Photo 4B).

Some quilters sign their name on the back of their quilts. This can be done in a variety of ways, including embroidery, cross stitch, and indelible ink (Figure 6.3). A history of the quilt can even be typed on muslin and sewn to or pieced into the backing. One more possibility: include a color photocopy of yourself or children for a special family quilt (Figure 6.4).

Some quilters back their quilts with plain white fabric because they feel it's more correct or traditional.

This is the safe way out. I imagine that white is often chosen by quilters who want their quilting stitches to be visible on the back. To me, the back is one of the last chances to make a design statement, and a big expanse of white is boring. I feel that a quilt backing should "go" with the front, but that it should also be a surprise. I spend lots of time looking for just the right backing for a particular quilt. Sometimes it's a fabric I wouldn't get the opportunity to use on the front, such as a large-scale print. If possible, in fact, I try not to have it appear on the front. For example, Foggy Day Leaves (Photo 12A) has a printed moire backing whose wavy lines suggest the fog to me. I have even been known to find a wonderful backing fabric in advance and to make a front to go with it.

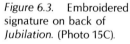

Figure 6.3. Embroidered signature on back of *Jubilation.* (Photo 15C).

Figure 6.4. Detail of color photocopy on back of quilt. Jane Toro, El Cerrito, CA.

A fascination with quilt bindings represents a fairly new area of interest to me. Historically, a simple solution was to bring the backing over to the front where it was turned under and stitched (Figure 6.5). Sometimes a piping was inserted. Another choice was to turn under the front and back towards each other and overcast (Figure 6.6). Or the edge would be bound with bias or straight-grain fabric (Figure 6.7). Tape bindings were commercially produced as well as being made at home on small hand-held looms. Fringes were also woven and netted for binding ornamentation.

My favorite binding method is the addition of a narrow fabric strip. I double the required width so it can be folded and sewn on double, giving it a richer feel. Whether it's on the bias or straight grain has more to do with appearance than ease of sewing. I only insist on a bias cut if a curve is involved in the edge. I also don't work with store-bought bias tape as I find it inferior in quality to the fabric I sew with.

The binding represents the absolute last chance to make a design statement. Spend the time to pick just the right accent to finish your quilt. Also, half the fun can come from being forced to substitute. It can be much more exciting than using the same fabric. This piecing can be in an erratic fashion as in Photo 15C, or related to the seams in the border as in Photo 13B. The piecing can be seamed with a straight or bias cut or both, as in Photo 13A.

Figure 6.5

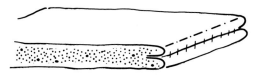

Figure 6.6

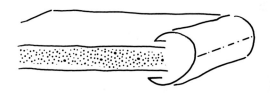

Figure 6.7

APPENDIX

A. Tea Dyeing

1 yard fabric
1 gallon water
4 tablespoons tea leaves
(or 4 tea bags)

Setting solution:
½ cup white vinegar
1 gallon water

1. Boil tea for 15 minutes; remove tea bags or leaves, straining if necessary.

2. Test four sample swatches of each fabric, simmering each in tea 15, 20, 25, and 30 minutes. Iron dry. Compare, and select best color.

3. Wet fabric. Simmer in tea solution for desired time.

4. Place fabric in setting solution for 10 minutes. Thoroughly rinse.

5. Further set color by drying fabric with iron or in clothes dryer.

B. Patching

METHOD I (Figure A.1)
1. Cut potential patch larger than necessary; iron under seam allowance on edge to be sewn.

2. Manipulate patch until a pleasing composition is achieved.

3. Sew. Trim away excess on patch and underneath patched area.

METHOD II (Figure A.2)
1. Join strips of varying width and angles together.

2. Cut desired shapes from patched fabric.

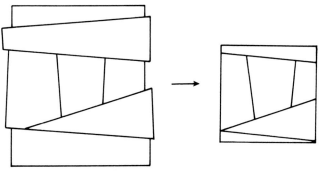

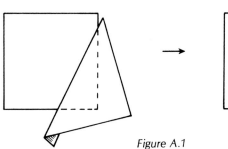 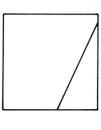

Figure A.1

Figure A.2

C. Joining Rows

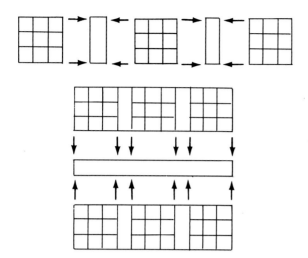

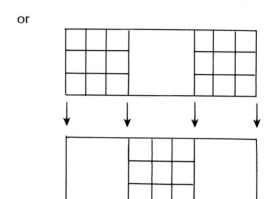

or

Figure A.3

D. Design Wall

Ideally you should be able to place fabric cut-outs on this surface and move them around easily until quilt design is composed. At this point fabric pieces should be pinned into position until sewing is completed.

1. Select fabric with a slight nap that cut-out shapes will adhere to easily. Possibilities include felt, flannel, Pellon Fleece™, Thermo Lamb™.

2. Install fabric, trying to keep it taut. Here are some possible approaches (Figure A.4):

   A. tack fabric permanently to wall

   B. form a frame with artists stretcher bars; tack fabric to this and hang from wall

   C. fold under and sew a narrow pocket at top and bottom of fabric; insert rods and hang construction from top rod

3. When a permanent installation is possible, there should be provision for pinning into the design wall. This can be achieved by first attaching a bulletin-board-like surface to the wall that will accommodate pins. The fabric is then tacked over this. Check at your lumber supply store for ideas for design wall materials. Celutex, an inexpensive insulation board, is one possibility.

A

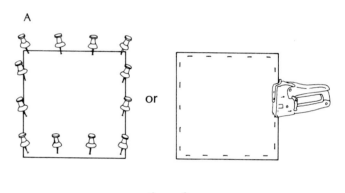

or

B

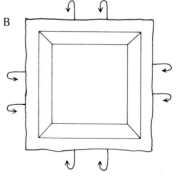

C

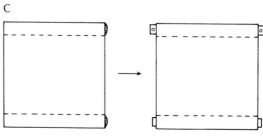

Figure A.4

BIBLIOGRAPHY

Bank, Mirra. *Anonymous Was a Woman.* New York: St. Martin's Press, 1979.

Clarke, Mary Washington. *Kentucky Quilts and Their Makers.* Lexington: University Press of Kentucky, 1976.

Conroy, Mary. *300 Years of Canada's Quilts.* Toronto: Griffin House, 1976.

Cooper, Patricia, and Buferd, Norma Bradley. *The Quilters, Women and Domestic Art.* Garden City, New York: Doubleday, 1977.

Dewhurst, C. Kurt, et al. *Artists in Aprons: Folk Art by American Women.* New York: Dutton, 1979.

Fennelly, Catherine. *Textiles In New England, 1790-1840.* Sturbridge, Massachusetts: Old Sturbridge Village, 1961.

Finley, Ruth E. *Old Patchwork Quilts and the Women Who Made Them.* Charles T. Branford Company, 1929.

Hall, Carrie, and Rose Kretsinger. *The Romance of the Patchwork Quilt in America.* New York: Bonanza Books, 1935.

Irwin, John Rice. *A People and Their Quilts.* Exton, Pennsylvania: Schiffer Publishing, 1983.

Johnson, Bruce. *A Child's Comfort: Baby and Doll Quilts in American Folk Art.* New York: Harcourt Brace Jovanovich, 1977.

Lithgow, Marilyn. *Quiltmaking and Quiltmakers.* New York: Funk and Wagnalls, 1974.

Mainardi, Patricia. *Quilts, The Great American Art.* San Pedro, California: Miles and Weir, 1978.

McKendry, Ruth. *Quilts and Other Bed Coverings in the Canadian Tradition.* Toronto: Van Nostrand Reinhold, 1979.

Nylander, Jane C. *Fabrics For Historic Buildings.* Washington, D.C.: Preservation Press, 1980.

Orlofsky, Patsy, and Myron Orlofsky. *Quilts in America.* New York: McGraw-Hill, 1974.

Pettit, Florence. *America's Printed and Painted Fabrics 1600–1900.* New York: Hastings House, 1970.

Woodard, Thos. K., et al. *Crib Quilts and Other Small Wonders.* New York: Dutton, 1981.

JAPANESE PATCHWORK

Edwards, Betty. *Drawing on the Right Side of the Brain.* Los Angeles: J. P. Tarcher, Inc., 1979.

Miyazaki, Emiko. *Beautiful Sashiko.* Tokyo: Japan Vogue, 1979. (In Japanese.)
　美しい刺し子, 宮崎恵美子著, 東京・日本ヴォーグ社刊, 1979年

Ota, Kimi. *Sashiko Quilting.* Seattle, Washington: Kimi Ota, 1981.

Sashiko. Tokyo: Japan Vogue, 1979. (In Japanese.)
　刺し子, 東京・日本ヴォーグ社刊, 1979年

Yoshida, Aiko. *Sashiko 100 Ways.* Tokyo: Bunko Shupan, 1981. (In Japanese.)
　刺し子百葉, 吉田英子著, 東京・文化出版局刊, 1981年

AFRO-AMERICAN QUILTS

Ferris, William. *Local Color: A Sense of Place in Folk Art.* New York: McGraw-Hill, 1982.

Freeman, Roland. *Something to Keep You Warm.* Jackson: Mississippi Department of Archives and History, 1981.

Picton, John, et al. *African Textiles.* London: British Museum Publications, 1979.

Price, Sally, and Richard Price. *Afro-American Arts of the Suriname Rain Forest.* Los Angeles: Museum of Cultural History, University of California, 1980.

Wahlman, Maude Southwell. *The Art of Afro-American Quiltmaking.* Bloomington: Indiana University Press, In Press.

Wahlman, Maude Southwell, et al. *Ten Afro-American Quilters.* Oxford: The Center for the Study of Southern Culture, University of Mississippi, 1983.